Crazier Than A Shithouse Rat

The Misadventures of a Bush Hippie

By Cliff Woffenden

Copyright 2020 by Cliff Woffenden

All rights reserved. No part of this book may be reproduced without permission in writing from the author, except by a reviewer.

Typesetting and graphics by the author.

Published by Howling Moon Productions
Box 223
Nakusp, B.C.
V0G 1R0

Canadian Cataloging in Publication Data
Woffenden, Cliff, 1946-
    Crazier Than a Shithouse Rat
    ISBN: 978-0-9694585-6-2

1. History 2. Autobiographical 3. My Life 1. Title.

ISBN: 978-0-9694585-6-2

Other Books by Cliff Woffenden:

But Now I See – a novel of alternative realities and shamanism

The Freedom of Responsibility – Spirituality and philosophy

A Pilgrim's Way - The Collected Works of

Ghost Peoples: The Sinixt, recovering from extinction – History of the local indigenous peoples.

Index

Index 4

Acknowledgments 7

Disclaimer 8

Introduction 9

Part 1

Arriving Here From There 10

Groovin' With the Guppies 14

Escaping the Matrix 19

Being Reborn 23

Part 2 – Tall Tales

Dealing With Fear of the Dark 27

Wingdam House 30

Dying On Your Own Terms 33

Redneck Hippies Shoot Back 35

Pat Loses His Cool 37

Northern Fried Chicken ………………….. 39

My First Winter Wood Gathering ….……. 41

Doug's Foul Mouthed Mynah Bird ….…… 44

Tom and Nancy …………………………… 47

Bullshit Jones and Don Quixote …………. 49

Dickey and Dorky…………………………. 51

Alice's Restaurant …………………….…... 53

My Telephone Service ……………………. 55

Exploding Barrel …………………………. 57

Exploding Swamp …………………...…… 59

Ron and the False Solomon Seal ….…....... 62

The Power of Water …………………….... 64

Goat Tales ………………………….…...... 65

Salmon Tales………………………….…... 75

Gnome Hunting …………………….……. 81

Department of Lands and Forests ….……. 83

Tough Love ……………………………..... 86

Bear and Fish Tales ……………………… 88

5

The Alternative Intentional Community …….. 95

The Teachings of Don Juan ………………... 107

Drafting for the Department of Holidays …… 109

Part 3

The Magic Of Morley …………………….. 112

The True Spirit of Christmas ………………… 122

The Birth of My Son ………………………….. 124

Postscript …………………………………… 126

Acknowledgments

I would like to thank all those people who helped me through all these adventures and helped me grow through all the weird and wonderful experiences of those heady days of life in the bush. Albert Lightning, Debby Plante, Marielle Gosslin, BJ Johnson, Dave Williamson, Reuben Gregor, Eagle Gosslin, Susan & Randy Horely, Victor Woffenden, Johnny Engro and many more who, knowingly or unknowingly, contributed to the great adventure.

A special thanks to Karen McMillan for her tireless and brutal proof reading skills. I am deeply grateful.

Disclaimer

Some may find Shithouse Rat irreverent or offensive. Although I do not set out to intentionally be so, it is a part of who I am. Expect me to be politically incorrect. Also expect to be offended once in a while. When it comes to humour, nothing is sacred and to me, life is nothing more than a Monty Python skit – the Ministry of Silly Walks.

Introduction

People have been asking me for a long time to write some of my stories down on paper. This has not been easy as most of the time it takes someone to trigger a memory. Just trying to remember on my own has proven difficult. It might have something to do with brain damage, but that involves many stories and I may get around to telling some of them in the process of writing this account of my earlier years.

I started this book about 10 years ago but ran into a mental block. I have not written anything since I had an attack of congestive heart failure at that time. Lately I have been micro dosing psilocybin mushrooms. It has cleared my mind and unlocked access to my memories. Looks like my mind has been cleared for takeoff. Yippy!!

Part 1

Arriving Here From There Without Getting Caught

A friend once said that the only difference between schizophrenics and the rest of us is that the rest of us had not been diagnosed yet.

Let's face it, from day one we are bombarded by the beliefs and neuroses of everyone around us until we really have no idea who we are. Most of us are so busy pretending to be normal or sane because we think that, if the rest of humanity really knew what was going on inside our heads, they would pump us full of drugs and lock us up in a padded cell. "They're coming to take me away Ha, Ha, Ho, Ho, Hee, Hee - to the Funny Farm..."

Well, guess what? I believe most of humanity feels like that, at least part of the time, because we really are all nuts.

Not one of us has had an identical experience of life. Not one of us is the same as any other in the way we see life/reality/truth/God/etc. because our experiences in life colour how we perceive those things. Some of us may agree on some things but none of us agrees on everything and therefore every one of us is different from everybody else. So, if this is so, just who is it who dictates what is normal or insane, by whom do they judge the rest of us and who appointed them an authority on the subject?

If you really stop and think about it, we are quite insane by definition simply because there is no such thing as normal or sane.

I once read the definition of insanity. They said it was the disbelief in the status quo version of reality. It made sense to me. I don't believe in it, so I must be insane. Actually, because of my experiences, I think anybody who accepts the status quo version is insane.

When I volunteered to work on the local Mental Health Clubhouse as the Public Relations dude, I was informed that the purpose of the clubhouse was to educate the public about mental illness and to try to remove some of the stigma prevalent in the public perception of mental heath issues. "Well", I said, rather seriously, "that should be easy. All I have to do is convince everybody they are crazy and then there would be no stigma."

Well, didn't all those mental health workers take offense to my words1 "You can't say that!" And all the crazy people said, "Why not? It's a perfectly good word."

When I told our local Mental Health officer what I thought about schizophrenia he replied, "and I will be getting around to diagnosing you soon!" Wow! Here is a guy who went to University to get a degree in "Sanity" so he could tell who was nuts and who wasn't - based on what? I want to know who wrote the curriculum. I want to know who thinks that they know more about this nut house than I do because I've been studying it for a lot longer than any of them and I think they are blowing hot air from where the sun don't shine.

The only real difference between me and thee is that I've come to accept my insanity. I am quite comfortable with it - Yea! - I'm proud of it. I wouldn't give it up for anything because it is who I am. I've earned these stripes and nobody is going to take them away.

What I have learned about life comes from a lifetime of weird, bizarre, and often hair-raising experiences that have made my hair fall out and my body to be mangled, but this has been one amazing journey from brain dead adolescent to a somewhat self-aware adult individual, who has a unique insight into his own and human behavior. That this unique perspective is probably of no use to anyone else is really no longer of much consequence to me.

Having said that, you might wonder why I bother to set this collection of personal stories to paper. For two reasons. 1: for my own entertainment and 2: for yours. Insanity is the only game in town, so sit back and enjoy the show because I plan to expose myself to you - to become the intellectual equivalent of a flasher.

Groovin' With the Guppies

It all began many, many years ago in the far off kingdom of Quee Bec, over the mountains and far, far away across the flat lands, on the other side of the Empire of On Tario where the frogs finally got smart and told the beaver clan to take a flying hike. As I have told many an astounded listener, who queried me about my origin, I was born in the biggest nut house in Canada - Montreal. Actually, I was born in a little hamlet on Montreal Island called Crawford Park (which probably bears a more frogish sounding name these days) next door to the infamous Douglas Hospital, which was the largest mental institute in post war Canada, Eh!

I was one of the original Baby Boomers, having been born nine months to the day after my dad returned from WWII. (I swear he jumped my mom right there on the dock.) Being the good Catholic he was, he decided to populate the planet with a whole bunch of little Catholic clones of himself. Although he wasn't as successful as the church would have liked, he managed to knock my mom up seven times, two of the would-be offspring consequently died at birth because my parents had incompatible blood types.

I understand that, at that time, the medical profession did not know how to circumvent that little genetic glitch and I came up two siblings short of what god had originally intended. I really didn't miss them since it was hard enough to fight my way to the feed trough as it was. (Hey! If you are looking for reverence, you are in the wrong book, Dude/tte.)

One of my first recollections of being conscious that I was on this planet was a reccurring nightmare of burning alive in a house fire. I would wake up screaming every night for months (or years). I was around 4 or 5 at the time.

The next thing I remember is that I am in a classroom full of similarly terrified kids being tortured by these sadistic penguins from hell called Nuns. Luckily we escaped their dementia when, for reasons that are unclear, it was decided to hire teachers from the outside world to terrorize us for the rest of our school daze instead.

Perhaps, at the time, they came to the realization that celibacy causes incredibly neurotic behavior in laboratory rats. Perhaps they thought that maybe, if they turned a bunch of loonies loose on us, who were supposedly having sex, we might get a more rounded education. Then again, perhaps that decision came from people who were celibate and therefore incapable of rational thought. Whatever!

As luck would have it, we moved to a small town fifteen miles off the island kingdom of Montreal to a town called Saint Bruno, where the frogs out numbered us ten to one. Consequently, there were only two rooms in the French elementary school for us underprivileged Anglos to get an education in. In one room you had grades one through four and in the other, grades five through seven.

There was no English Catholic High School in town. When I failed grade seven, due to neglect on the teachers part, and a complete lack of interest on my part, I persuaded my father to send me over to the Protestant school. There they promptly put me in grade eight as a reward for escaping the Draconian warlords over at the system run by the Scarlet Whore of Revelations.

The inmates at this asylum were much more open-minded and I received a rather liberal education compared to what I would have, had I stayed at the "Ho's" house of ill repute. At the time I had no idea that I was to become the rebel that I was becoming.

In retrospect, I must thank my dad for planting the seeds of rebellion in me with his fascist style of Catholic/military child rearing. If it hadn't been for his constant reminder that I was a useless tit and as dumb as a sack of hammers, I would never have tried to set out to prove him wrong. Unfortunately, he died before I realized that he was right. But I did become a rebel and I suppose that could be considered an accomplishment in itself, depending on your particular perspective on things.

I heard, in my wild and rebellious youth, that Buckminster Fuller once said that he was never a radical in his youth for fear he would become conservative in his old age. Too late! I have had to be very diligent in keeping an eye out for any conservative leanings that have tried to infiltrate my mind so as to keep my radical view of life and reality. God forbid that I should ever become anal retentive like so many others I grew up with.

My school years were a blur of disinterest except for dancing, which I became proficient at as a matter of survival. In my freshman year I was involved in sports because it was part of the curriculum. I did not enjoy body slams since most of them were aimed at me because I was of a diminutive body size. I also did not get off on snapping wet towels in the locker room showers or other forms of pissing contests indulged in by pubescent boys.

One day, while getting my body pounded on the football field, I noticed that the girls were always sitting up on the bleachers watching the show. I decided then and there that sitting with the girls would be much more fun than having pain inflicted on me by all these big, bum slapping, repressed homosexuals on the field. So I joined the girls and lived happily, and painlessly, for the rest of my school daze.

While the jocks were getting their rocks off on socially accepted groping during sports, I learned to be the best damn dancer that town had ever known. I excelled to the point where my entire record collection consisted of dance contest winnings. I became very popular with the ladies because they wanted free records, too.

The jocks became very jealous of me and one time, at the local strip mall, several of the bigger boys grabbed me, hoisted me on their shoulders and carted me off between two buildings. Their intention, they said, was to strip off my clothes and turn me loose in the middle of the parking lot. I got such a terrified rush of adrenaline that I kicked the hell out all four guys before I even hit the ground. They never bothered me again. The word went out to not mess with Woffenden "because he is crazier than a shithouse rat."

Unfortunately, part of my other survival character development was to become a dickhead like most of the jocks. I thought that by picking on the more timid that I would be more socially accepted into a wider range of high school cliques. The strategy worked but I was losing my self-respect because being an asshole was not compatible with my aspirations in life: the main one being to just be a good person.

This led to the downward spiral into alcohol abuse and becoming an even bigger dickhead. After graduation I got into this career big time. I was drunk for most of the next four years, so what I remember is pretty much disgusting behavior until everything went out of focus and then waking up with my head in a toilet bowl.

Fortunately for me, a friend came back from college in New Brunswick about 1968 and turned me on to Vitamin "L" (LSD for you uninitiated). My first trip exposed to me what an asshole I had become and led to the realization that I really didn't like alcohol or being drunk. The only reason I drank was because I couldn't stand my friends when they were drunk unless I was. It never occurred to me to change friends since most everybody I knew got drunk on a regular basis.

Escaping the Matrix.

When I graduated from high school, my dad took me by the hand, led me to the employment office of Northern Electric and said, "Sign him up." I didn't figure it out till 4 years later that my meteoric rise through the ranks was engineered by my dad, who was a lifer with the company. Northern Electric became Northern Telecom and later Nortel.

I was sitting at my desk one day when I had an epiphany: I looked around at the guys who had been there for thirty to forty years and I saw myself in thirty years sitting at the same desk and my mind revolted. I kicked over my desk, jumped up, gave my boss the Italian salute for "Up Yours!" and walked out of the building. Thus began my extrication from the Matrix. It didn't happen over night but I set the trajectory and there was no going back.

The first acid trip came a little while later. It was only a quarter hit but I liked it a lot. I realized that it could really mess me up if I didn't treat it with the utmost respect. So I decided to treat it as a sacrament. Before every trip I would do a little ritual and plan where I wanted to explore, set the atmosphere and choose the participants to join me on the journey.

It was after a few of these trips that I realized that what I was doing was breaking down the barriers set up by my social conditioning. As Terence McKenna later said, "your culture is not your friend". It took almost two hundred such journeys to finally break free of the mind numbing, mental, and psychic prison that my upbringing had imposed on me. All the while, I was exploring new territory, delving into the depths of the human psyche that I never knew existed.

I zoomed into the atomic structure of a dead bumblebee and walked out into the outer reaches of our solar system, I have "seen" the energy of all living things beyond their material illusions, felt that energy merge with mine, communicated with many forms of wildlife from bugs to plants to animals, shared Love with a goddess, joined my soul with another in a realm beyond the physical; pure energy, formless, and divine.

I became aware of what is real and understood that, what most people call reality is a lie of biblical proportions; a program of the mind designed to keep us from the truth of who and what we are. We are gods and goddesses, co-creators of the world we inhabit. We are no less than the human eyes and ears of the Universe, made of the same stuff as the Universe, filled with the same creative, conscious energy that is the All That Is. Our core, our center, is the conscious energy that animates the vehicle that we inhabit, our bodies.

This revelation led me to realize that we are spirit first, physical beings second. Quantum physics says that there is no material without an observer. We are that observer. That what we call matter is nothing more than low frequency energy compressed. We have been stuck in the lie of the material world for eons and one of our purposes for choosing to incarnate on this plane of existence is to get back to who and what we really are; spiritual beings, conscious energy, and that all spiritual paths are fingers pointing the way to this truth.

But the LSD experience is transitory. It allows you to peek at the possibilities that await us on the other side of the veil of lies. It gives you a window, but not a door. Every trip ends with a return to the Matrix. You come "down" to the lie but you are motivated to find the door and to step through it. Psychedelics cannot take us there. That is the next part of the journey. That journey becomes our life's path, the path less traveled.

So I set off on an adventure without a clue or map on how to get there, just an overwhelming need to find what is real. I wasn't aware, at the time, that I had guides. I would meet them along the way. My intention was not to follow the dream so much as to find out what the dream was. I instinctively knew that the answers were to be found in nature, so I set off for a new life with no vision or plan: nothing more than blind faith that I was headed in the right direction.

In 1972, my brother and I purchased an old GMC van and left Montreal, heading west to discover our destiny. As luck would have it, we ended up in a place called Cottonwood House, on the Barkerville highway, east of Quesnel, BC. We found an old school buddy of ours there who owned some property and we were welcome to stay there until we got our bearings. As we drove into his driveway, I had a distinct feeling of coming home. That is when my new life began, when I went from being an urban hippie to a Bush Hippie Living the Life.

That, of course, is the next bit.

Being Reborn

When I left Montreal, I wanted to be more involved with the processes of life: instead of turning on a tap or flipping a light switch, I wanted to experience getting my own water and producing my own power, building my own home, and furnishing it with my own creations. I wanted to be involved in the processes of my life. In other words, I wanted to create a life that was a living work of art. It was a big dream considering I worked in an office up until then. I had no skills in carpentry, mechanics, plumbing, or electricity but I was determined.

So here I am, a big city boy out in the wilderness without a clue. Now what? Well, I can't go back to the asylum, so it is do or die. Fortunately, I am not the only urban refugee that arrives here at around this time. Over the course of the next few months, approximately forty other similarly clueless hippies find their way from various parts of Canada and the US, to this remote place and through chance meetings, we made an agreement to help each other survive.

At first, my brother and I stay at our friend's house. He had a twenty five acre piece of land and on it was an old log cabin built during the dirty thirties. It was a rather crude and tiny cabin that desperately needed some TLC. This eventually became our base of operations. It had no running water or power, which suited me fine but not my brother so much.

For me, this was such an adventure that I couldn't wait to get up in the morning and go exploring my new surroundings. I spent weeks wandering around in the forest observing nature up close and personal. I traveled with only an old 8mm movie camera and filmed beavers building dams, elk grazing in remote meadows, moose eating in large ponds, Ruffed Grouse and their chicks foraging in the forest. I never carried a weapon of any sort, which caused some consternation among some friends.

I would fish down on the river and many times shared my fishing hole with black bears. I would have long conversations with them. I never felt threatened. I found wildlife better company than most humans. Towns folk would ask, "aren't you afraid of bears?" I would say, "No. Bears have no hidden agendas or ulterior motives. They are just busy being bears. Humans, on the other hand, are unpredictable and dangerous."

Eventually, I convinced an old friend, a beautiful young French Canadian lady, to join my in my adventure. We lived in my friend's cabin for about a year before we decided we needed a place of our own.

I found an abandoned tool shed from a long ago placer gold mine and decided to take up residence. The Cottonwood River flowed by and that was to become our "running water" source (I had to run down to the river with two five gallon buckets to get my water). Of course, there was no electricity, no phone, TV, radio, rent, or utility bills to pay. I heated with wood and found an old wood cookstove in an abandoned cabin downriver and some kerosene lamps for light.

I was so broke that I had to use cardboard boxes to stuff between the studs for insulation. I salvaged some wood from a derelict bunkhouse, ten miles up the road, to finish the inside, and cut some dead pine trees to add a log bedroom. The following year, I added a kitchen with the wood cook stove I found. Over the years I added more rooms, a shed and a sauna/workshop to the collection. It turned out to be quite a comfortable abode as things progressed.

Living (squatting, actually) in the forest is not for the faint of heart and is frowned upon by those who think they are the government. Although considered illegal, this country was built by squatters and is written into the BNA act, but that is a tale for later.

One would think that a person of sound mind and body would think twice about uprooting oneself from "civilization" to go live in the forest, without much experience in such endeavors, but fortunately, I was neither. Most people would think that, after 200+ LSD trips, my mind would be quite fried and perhaps they are right. But I could no longer participate in that particular brand of insanity that civilization had to offer and I had become quite accustomed to my own insanity.

    Due to lack of skills and a natural born clumsiness, my life became a series of hair-raising experiences mixed with some magic and beautiful encounters with Mother Natures' finest. So, from here on in, I will tell stories of what it was like to be a fish out of water, so to speak.

Part 2

Tall Tales

Dealing With Fear of the Dark

When I first moved to the bush, I was living in an old ten by ten foot log cabin built during the great depression. It had no electricity or running water. I was using a kerosene lamp for light. When I went outside to pee, I realized true darkness for the first time in my life. When you live in a city, it is never really dark. I looked up and could see billions of stars, but on nights when it was cloudy or moonless, it was very, very dark. It was so dark that I couldn't see my own hand fumbling with my zipper. Then there was a noise and I almost jumped out of my skin.

I realized that, if I were going to live this lifestyle, I would have to overcome this paralyzing fear. I had a friend who lived in a similar cabin five miles down the road, just off the Barkerville highway, so I decided that I would go visit him and stay until it got dark. I didn't have a vehicle at the time, so I had to walk. Five miles doesn't seem like a very long way, but in the dark, believe me, it is.

So I am walking along for maybe a few hundred feet when I hear what sounded like a monster scream off in the bushes near by. I went into complete panic mode and started running with a full on adrenaline rush. I ran all the way back to my cabin. As I reached the door, I reached out to open it and ran straight into the outside edge of the door with my forehead, knocking me out cold. When I woke up, it was morning. I was still lying on the ground outside my cabin with a huge goose egg on my forehead.

The next evening, I returned to my friend's cabin and repeated the exercise. I did that for several weeks, until I could walk home without getting the shit scared out of me. I doubt that I was in any real danger, but my big city mind, which is and has always been, rather imaginative, created the danger from unknown sounds. Eventually I could recognize most of the sounds and the fear went away.

A year or so later, I was visiting another friend who had a cabin next to the highway about two and a half miles down the road, about a third of a mile past the Cottonwood bridge. There was a rock bluff that was created when they blasted through a large rock outcropping to make the right of way for the highway. I had to walk through there on my way home.

I was passing under the rock wall, about midnight, when I heard a cougar scream, right over my head. There is no mistaking that scream, I tell you. The next thing I know is I am sitting at my friend's kitchen table. He was washing dishes in the sink when he turned around to get something and jump, startled to see me there.

"Where the hell did you come from?" he shouted. (I was as white as a ghost.) I couldn't speak at first. I couldn't remember running back to his place. I don't know how I got there. I just remember the cougar scream and the next thing I was sitting at his table. The only thing I could think of was that somehow I projected my body out of harm's way. I still think that is what I did. There is no logical explanation other than that. I believe it may have been my first shamanic experience.

Wingdam House

A Tale of Eight Hippies

In the fall of 1973, a bunch of Hippies from Mission, BC arrived in our neck of the woods led by a guy who was to become my best friend for life. Up the Barkerville Highway, east of where I was situated at Cottonwood, BC, there was an abandoned mining site called Wingdam. At this site was a two story abandoned mansion and these newly arrived Hippies decided it would be a good idea to resurrect this abandoned house so they could have a place to winter.

On the first floor was a huge kitchen, about twenty by twenty foot, and dining area with a walk-in fireplace. Down the hall were four or five bedrooms. So they moved in. The second story was way more space than they needed, so they closed it off. The first night they were unable to sleep. Seems that the traffic up on the second floor was like downtown traffic in a major city. Packrats were running amok. So two of these big city hippies decided to take a flash light and a 22 rifle up there to see if they could slow them down some.

They sat in the dark for a bit and when the running around started up again, they flipped on the light, the rifle rang out and a packrat fell dead. They turned off the light and waited for the next round. In a matter of seconds the traffic started up again, the light went on and another rat was dead. This went of for a while until they realized that there were so many rats that they would be up there shooting for days.

A new plan was hatched. The next day they went to Quesnel and bought some rat poison. They set it up in daylight. That night the running around seemed to peter off by midnight and they got a good night's sleep. The snows came and they were cozy in their mansion.

Around Easter, I was visiting, sitting around the dining room table enjoying a cuppa java with friends, when there came a horrifying scream from down the hall. We all ran down to see what the commotion was. We entered one of the bedrooms to see someone with the covers pulled up over her head. She was pointing down toward the middle of the pure white bedspread. We looked closer and saw the whole top of the bed was squirming with maggots.

At first she had thought the roof was leaking. It was spring and since she had not been up yet, didn't know it was sunny out. It appears that all those frozen, poisoned rats had thawed out and were decaying in the floor above and their decaying flesh had produced a real swarm of maggots. They were dropping down from the ceiling like rain. It didn't take them long to pack and get the hell out of there.

Dying On Your Own Terms

Ron Whitman was an old hermit that lived at Wingdam just up the road from the Wingdam house. When I first met this man, I was annoyed at how fast and nervously he spoke. But then I noticed there was a strange tone in his voice.

Later, I learned he had been caught between a loading ramp and a truck. His body was nearly cut in two at the waist. Somehow he was patched back together and had lived alone for the past thirty years in excruciating pain. Yet, not once did he ever mention it or complain. He was so happy to just wake up each day that he was not going to let it get him down.

Ron lived with his four half-wolf dogs. He told us on several occasions that when he died, he wanted his dogs to eat him - his last gift to them for their unwavering friendship.

On Christmas day, 1974, we planned a large feast at the Wingdam house. A friend, Rick, was supposed to pick Ron up and bring him over. When Rick arrived, he was alone and informed us that Ron was in the process of fulfilling his last wish - his last Christmas present to his four faithful companions.

We all gathered around the banquet table, raised our glasses of wine in honour of Ron's spirit and wished him our best. His painful ordeal was over. He died in his home, as humble as it was, and he had the chance to fulfill his final wish. We were happy for him.

Three days later, we informed the authorities. They were not impressed. They made sure that Ron had also been the dogs' last supper. We all knew, as did Ron, that this would happen. After tasting human flesh, there was no way that those half-wolf dogs could be controlled.

Redneck Hippies Shoot Back

Baker Lake is a small lake right beside the Barkerville Highway. There was an old log cabin there that was built by the first doctor in the area. It had long been abandoned, so, like many other abandoned cabins, a bunch of hippies moved in, in the early seventies. One of those hippies was a fellow named Pat, who was an ex-junkie. One day, the guys decided to go hunting for deer. The girls stayed back to do some canning.

At some point in the afternoon, a bunch of redneck goons pulled up outside the cabin and started shooting at it. The girls all hit the floor, terrified. Eventually, they left. Soon after, Pat and the boys returned from hunting to find the girls still lying on the floor. They were afraid to get up. Pat looked around and saw all the bullet holes in the cabin and most of the windows were blown out.

Pat, not one to shy away from a fight, recruited a bunch of neighbouring hippies with guns, loaded them into his truck and headed to Quesnel. When they arrived, the guys in the back of the truck stood up and positioned their rifle butts on their hips. They drove slowly up and down every street in town to let everybody know that redneck hippies shoot back. We didn't have much trouble after that.

Pat Loses His Cool

I was at a campfire party one night, which were quite common at the time. I got royally drunk. I was sitting on a bench about ten to twelve feet from the fire. Behind me and to my right was a rather large fir tree. Standing by the fire was Pat and another fellow I will call Brian because I forget his name. Pat had his back to me and Brian was facing in my direction.

Pat was a bit homophobic and he thought Brian was gay. Brian denied it vehemently. They were in a heated argument about it when, through the haze of my inebriation, I heard Pat say, "Oh Yah, well prove it." The next thing I see is Brian pull down his zipper and flip out his penis.

Pat reached out and grabbed hold of Brian's penis and pulled on it as hard as he could. I swear it stretched out about twenty four inches or more before Brian was forced to follow its trajectory. Pat literally threw Brian through the air, over his shoulder, toward me.

Brian's right shoulder hit my right shoulder and I fell back off the bench onto my back. Brian was thrown head first into the fir tree. He landed beside me in a crumpled heap. He rolled over and looked me in the eye, raised his bottle of beer and said, "I didn't spill a drop."

I suddenly became very sober. Brian got up and went back to the fire. I got up and went home. That was a little too intense for me. As I drove away, I saw Pat and Brian were still arguing.

Northern Fried Chicken

One evening a friend and I were heading home from Quesnel and decided to have a bite to eat in an all-night diner out on Two Mile Flat. It was one of those retro diners with a row of round stools at the serving counter and some square booths. The stools were all full of mill workers, so we slipped into one of the booths, close to the exit.

An indigenous man walked in to order some fried chicken to go. While he was waiting for his order, the mill workers were harassing him, calling him all kinds of racially derogatory names and slurs. I was about ready to say something about what a bunch of assholes they were when the indigenous man turned to them and said, "You just wait and see, when the East Indians take over this town, they're gonna treat you like shit." He turned, after receiving his order and walked out. My friend and I gave him a standing ovation as he walked out the door. "Bravo! Bravo!"

Well, the town was taken over by East Indians but that was after I moved down to the West Kootenays, so I don't know if they are treating the rednecks like shit or not.

My First Winter Wood Gathering

    I didn't own a chainsaw that first winter. All I had was a Swede Saw, a bow shaped saw with a blade something like a hacksaw. It was about twenty inches long. Oh, and a double-bladed axe.

    Before the snows came, it rained for weeks. I went to bed one night in the rain and woke up to 3 or 4 feet of new snow and -10 Celsius. It snowed for a month or so, with an accumulation of about twenty feet by New Years.

    What was interesting about that year was the fact that the ground never froze. This caused the snow to melt up from the ground, creating a hollow of a few feet beneath the snow on top. I could walk on the surface of the snow with snowshoes but there was enough snow that I didn't sink down. But every time I took a step, I could feel several feet of snow drop down into the hollow below. A loud rumble would accompany it. It made me feel like the Golly Green Giant.

My partner, Marielle, arrived from Montreal in the middle of January. My dog, Caesar, was a little jealous at first but he soon warmed up to her. They became inseparable. They both helped with the wood gathering.

I rigged up an 8-foot toboggan with side rails made of one by twos so we could haul a decent amount of firewood out of the bush. The first tree I tried to fell landed in the crotch of another tree about twenty feet up. The butt sprang up just past my face, went about forty feet in the air and came down within inches of my face. I was wearing snowshoes and couldn't move fast enough to get out of its way. That is why they call those types of trees widow makers.

My snowshoes were the old wooden type with rawhide webbing and a tail out the back. I loaded the wood on the sleigh, used a horse halter as a harness on Caesar and told him to go home. He looked at me like I had lost my mind. So I tied a rope to the front of his halter and started to pull him down the trail. At first he just sat there and refused to budge, then reluctantly began to walk. He soon figured out that the faster he moved, the easier it was to pull. Soon he was running on the narrow path with me trying to stay ahead of him.

That was difficult to do with snowshoes on and he began to gain on me. After a hundred feet or so, he stepped on the tail of my snowshoes and I fell hard, face down into the snow. By now he was moving pretty fast and dragged the toboggan right over me with that load of wood, pushing my face deeper into the snow. I was able to pull my face up just as he arrived at the cabin. Marielle was standing there, watching the whole debacle, laughing her head off.

    I made my way to the cabin and we decided we needed to refine our plan. I got out a bunch of Milk Bones from the box, gave Marielle some and I put some in my pocket. I led Caesar back out to the woodpile and gave him a bone. I loaded up the toboggan and whistled to Marielle to call him. He ran to her and she gave him another bone while she unloaded. When she was done, she whistled to me to call him back out. The operation went amazingly smooth once we got the hang of it.

Doug's Foul Mouthed Mynah Bird

Doug was local a stone carver who taught me how to carve soapstone. He had a little touristy craft shop by the highway that passed through Cottonwood village site. The highway eventually bypassed the village and he closed up shop soon after.

He bought the place from a little old lady who owned a Mynah bird that was almost as old as she was. He inherited the bird with the property. He purchased the house and land and then built his little shop in front of the house.

When the old lady lived there, a lot of old hermits used to come out of the bush and stop by for tea and cookies from time to time. The Mynah bird lived in a cage in the living room. The old men would strike up a conversation with the bird that picked up sayings from them. The bird knew several dozen sayings that it spoke with their voices. That is how we figured there were several dozen visitors who had tea with the old lady.

One day, Doug came home with a cassette recorder and decided to test it out by recording the bird talking. (I can only remember one of its sayings: "What did you say that was so valuable.") Doug turned on the recorder and started talking to the bird and it went off on a tangent. It went through almost its entire repertoire of sayings in one long spiel.

Doug rewound the cassette and pressed play. Well, the bird went completely berserk, screeching, flapping its wings and slamming into the sides of the cage. Doug turned off the recorder and it calmed down. After that, it never said another word except "Fuck You!"

A Mynah bird's mating call is a wolf whistle. It can wolf whistle in a number of different ways, from soft and sexy to a loud, high pitched screech that will make your ears bleed. That is the only other sound it would make after "the incident".

Doug had to go away for three weeks in the middle of tourist season and asked if I could mind his shop. On sunny days I would hang the bird's cage out on the deck. The bird could not see into the shop from where it hung but somehow it knew if people went in and bought something or not. When they would leave the shop after buying something it would give them a wolf whistle and if they didn't, it would say, "Fuck You!"

I can't tell you how many times it had its picture taken be cause it said "Fuck You." Mom, pop and the kids would be walking down the steps when it would blast them. Mom would inevitably say, "Oh look George, the bird can talk. Take its picture." It was the most photographed thing in all of Cottonwood. I would give him a treat after ever time. Eventually, I grew to despise tourists as much as the bird did. By the time Doug returned, I was ready to shoot them all.

Tom and Nancy

Tom and Nancy lived in a little cabin by a lake across the highway from Baker Lake. It was probably part of Baker at one time but the highway cut through it. Tom fancied himself a bushman and a great white hunter. Nancy was a very pretty little blond less than five foot tall and maybe eighty pounds. The cabin was down a small hill from the logging road that went by it.

One night Nancy was out at dusk when she noticed some headlights up on the road, near where they kept their truck. She got paranoid that someone was stealing their battery from the truck, so she call Tom and he came out with his Winchester rifle. He ran up to the road, yelling at the people to get lost. When he arrived on the road, they were already racing away toward the highway. All he could see was their taillights so he started pumping bullets between them. (Yah, Tom was crazy too).

    The next morning, Tom decided to go hunting and left Nancy sitting in the cabin alone. She eventually heard a vehicle pull up on the road and feared the guys from the night before had returned to seek revenge. She sat on her bed a shook in fear. Turned out it was Pat, (the ex-junkie). He knocked on the door but she didn't answer. Pat did not like Tom much and thought he would play a practical joke on him. He entered the cabin and saw Nancy sitting on the bed in total fear.

    He asked her what was wrong and she told him the story of the previous night. Pat looked around and saw Tom's shotgun. He walked over to it, chambered a round and handed it to Nancy. He told her to shoot the next person to walk through the door and left her there, holding the gun. As Pat had hoped, Tom was the first person to come through the door. Lucky for all of them, Nancy didn't shoot Tom, although she came within a hair of doing so.

Bullshit Jones and Don Quixote

Bullshit Jones was a gold miner who lived across the Cottonwood River a few miles from where I lived. To get to his place, I had to cross the river in my truck via an old wagon crossing. The water was shallow and wide there.

Bullshit was called that because he was full of it. He would con a bunch of investors to invest in his mine under false pretenses. He would arrange for them to come out to his claim and on the morning before their arrival he would go down to the river with his shotgun and a shell full of gold nuggets and shoot it into the bank of the river.

When the suckers arrived, he would take them down to the riverbank, at the spot he had shot, and dig out a shovel of gravel and run it thought his gold pan. They were all very impressed at the sight of all that colour and would hand over their hard earned cash. Then he would go out and get severely drunk. He kept doing that until one day he ended up dead.

I was over on that side of the river one day, a few months after his demise, when I dropped into his cabin. Most of his stuff had been pilfered, all except a 1880ish version of Don Quixote with a messed up cover and his wood cookstove. The book was full of Dore original woodcut drawings. They were magnificent, so I took it home.

I eyeballed the stove, because I didn't have one, but left it there to discuss it with my wife. I later returned to pick it up. It was completely black, covered in soot and grease. It took me many days to clean it up but the finished product was stunning: chrome trim, cream enamel on the doors and the rest black. The firebox and oven were in great shape too. Marielle became a master at using it. I even built a kitchen, in the new cabin (at the time), to house it.

I told my dad about the book one time, in a letter. He said he knew someone who could repair the cover so I sent it to him. I never saw it again. Life got real busy and I forgot about the book until recently when a friend said something about Don Quixote. My dad died almost 30 years ago, so I still don't know what happened to it.

Dickey and Dorky

Dickey and Dorky lived next to the Barkerville Highway at Mosquito Flats, just across the river from our place. Their driveway came off the highway on a steep decline. Across from their cabin was an old barn and beside that was their outhouse. The outhouse was built on top of a hill that went down to the river. The front of the outhouse was a straight walk in but the back was on stilts because it was up in the air. Some of the boards at the back, on the downhill side, were missing.

    One morning Dorky was out in the outhouse with her cup of coffee having her morning constitutional, when she heard a noise coming from below her. She rose up a little to look down the hole when she saw a bear having itself a warm breakfast of Dorky's latest deposit. She started screaming for Dickey to come out to the outhouse. Dickey had his shotgun and fired off a blast to scare the bear, which it did. After that, Dickey had to ride shotgun outside the outhouse every time Dorky need to use it.

That first winter, I was keeping my goat kids in their barn. Around the beginning of February, we began to hear a lot of coyotes yipping at night. It was a little disconcerting, as the goats were quite vulnerable in that dilapidated old barn.

Dicky and Dorky had driven out to BC on a BSA motorcycle. Dickey decided to take the headlight off the bike and mount it on a pole, hook a battery up to it, and a switch to turn it on. He wanted to know how many coyotes were out there because it sure sounded like a lot.

That night, there was a terrible racket going on out there, so Dickey turned on his headlight that was facing away from the road toward the back of the property. When the light went on, we saw at least a hundred pairs of red eyes looking back at us from the tree line. That was a little unnerving, to say the least.

This posed a big problem for me and my goats. The next morning I was out in the barn reinforcing the structure to make it more coyote proof. We found out later that the coyotes gathered there, every February, to mate. They weren't very interested in eating anything. They only had one thing on their minds.

Alice's Restaurant

One Christmas, we were invited to a friend's place for dinner on his trap line 20 miles away. As we were snowed in pretty good and had accumulated a fair amount of garbage, I decided to load up the toboggan with big green garbage bags and pull them out to the truck, since we had to drive by the Cottonwood dump, anyway. When we got to the dump, it was closed and had not been plowed out all winter. That pissed me off, since there was a highways gravel pit right next to it.

Anyway, we went to BJ's trap line and had a great feast of wild game meat and stuff. When we went to leave, I discovered that his hound had jumped into the back of our truck and tore all the garbage apart. What a mess! What to do?

On the way back, I stopped at the gravel pit. I decided to leave a message for those lazy pricks and dump my garbage in the entrance. I had my friend stand behind the truck to make sure there was no incriminating evidence be left behind. Turns out, he missed one.

One bright early sunny spring morning I looked out the window of our bedroom and saw an RCMPeep ossifer trudging through the snow holding a clipboard. I knew what it was right away and said to Marielle, "shades of Alice's Restaurant."

Sure enough, he had a garbage-encrusted envelope, with my name on it, attached to his clipboard. I'm no good at lying so I told him the truth. He said the Department of Holidays wanted to prosecute me for my heinous crime. After hearing my pitiful story, he ended up giving me a $25 ticket for littering. I know it doesn't sound like much to most people but to a dirt-poor bush hippie, it was a lot of groceries down the tubes in 1975.

My telephone service

We had friends living on the other side of the river at Mosquito Flats. To get their attention, when I wanted to talk to them about something, I would climb up onto my roof with my 12 gauge shotgun and fire a blast up into the air. Randy would climb up onto his roof and we would yell back and forth at each other. We didn't use it very often but it served our purpose.

One morning I woke up to a pair of game wardens, plowing through knee deep, wet snow, coming to pay us a visit. One was young but the other was an overweight, older fellow that I recognized as the head warden. I had talked to him a few times and he recognized me.

He made small talk for a while but I began to notice that his accompanying Malamute companion was running all over the place, sniffing all over. I also began to notice that the warden was giving him rather discreet hand signals. I finally asked him what he was looking for.

He told me that someone had complained to his office that I was shooting moose out of season. I laughed. He asked me what was so funny. I told him about my telephone system. I showed him my shotgun and how the barrel was so pitted it wasn't good for anything else.

I would never hunt out of season because of something Bob Dylan once said: "It takes an honest man to live outside the law."

There was a trail across the river that was compact ice. It was early spring and the water was rising. It was melting on top of the winter's ice on the river. The water was lapping at both sides of the trail that was only an inch or two above the water level and getting narrower by the day. It was like walking a tightrope.

The old guy was huffing and puffing from the walk down and he told his assistant to cross the river, get their vehicle, drive down to our cabin and pick him up. It was funny watching the younger man try to navigate the trail. I had stopped using it a few days earlier. He kept slipping off and getting his feet wet. Once he managed to get across, he had to hike a few miles to get back to their truck.

Eventually, he was able to drive down, with much struggling, in the knee deep, wet spring snow. He didn't bother getting out of the truck. The old man got in and they struggled to turn it around and drive back up the steep hill they came down on.

All in all, it was a very entertaining encounter with the law, although I don't think they were amused.

Exploding Barrel

While living at the cabin on the Cottonwood River, I decided I needed to produce some electricity using methane to run a generator. I had been using kerosene lamps for four years or more and thought I was pushing my luck. A slight bump of a table and the cabin would have been burnt to the ground in about five minutes.

To accomplish this feat of genius, I rigged up a 50 gallon barrel to put some grass clipping and goat shit into, painted it flat black so the sun would heat it up to perking temperature, rigged a small gas engine to run on methane (rejetted the carburetor) and hooked it all up to a skidder inner tube as the holding vessel.

The idea was simple: store the methane in the tube, when the pressure built up, release the gas to the carburetor, and run the engine that would turn an alternator from an old car, and charge a battery.

I had used the barrel for gas to run my truck previously, so I had to get rid of any residual gas before putting in the slurry to produce methane. I filled up the barrel with water and flushed it out three times. When I was done, I decided that I better make sure the gas was all gone, so I pulled out my trusty Bic and flicked it over the bung hole.

Well, there was a huge boom and a column of flame shot about three hundred feet into the air. I was thrown backwards until the wall of my sauna suddenly halted my trajectory. As I slid down the wall onto the ground, I noticed Marielle looking out the kitchen window at me, shaking her head as if to say, "you bloody idiot."

Undaunted by this setback, I pushed ahead. I filled the barrel with slurry, hooked up the copper pipes and valves and waited for the sun to come out. Weeks later it still had not stopped raining so I built a small greenhouse over the barrel. The sun never did come out that summer, so the experiment failed.

I ended up using my '48 Mercury pickup to charge the battery. I hooked up the battery to some $2 tail light fixtures I bought to light up our cabin.

Exploding swamp.

　　Some friends and I bought a hundred and six acres of land thirty miles up a logging road and three miles back in the bush. There were three streams running through it, all coming together at the place where it left the property. There was a beaver pond there too. The beavers would flood the meadows (there were four of them created by the streams). Anyway, we had to let out the water so we could mow the hay, which meant breaking the beaver dam, two weeks before haying could begin. Since it was close to my house, I started the project, which proved to be easier said than done. I'd spend a good part of the day tearing the dam apart and they would spend all night building it back up.
　　After a couple of weeks, the hole in the dam kept getting smaller, the pile of debris kept getting bigger and I was running out of places to throw the wood. It was kind of cramped in there, as the trees did not leave much room

to move. Anyway, I decided that I needed to get rid of the pile.

It was very hot that day and I was a little groggy. In my stupor, I decided to throw some gas on the pile. I looked around and saw a small log laying down, crossing the stream just below the dam so, having watched too many Hollywierd movies, I threw most of the gas on the pile, which was on one side of the stream, and ran a bead of gas across the log to the other side. I envisioned lighting the bead on my side and watching it flow along the log to the pile of debris, where it would ignite the way it does in the movies.

That, of course, is not how those things work. In the movies, I found out later, they use kerosene not gas and that is why it flows slowly along the ground before there is a big Kaboom!!! Did I mention it was a very hot, sunny day? Well, I lit a match with the intention of throwing it down to start my slow burn to the pile, when there was a very loud boom as the evaporated gas ignited as soon as the match caught fire.

Luckily there was a small tree right behind me that was flexible enough to let me fall back onto the ground and then push me back up into a standing position again.

My ears were ringing like a five alarm fire. As I stood there dazed and confused, I could barely hear voices off in the distance yelling, "What the fuck was that?" and "Are you OK?" Apparently, the other members of our little communal property heard my failed experiment from the other side of the property.

Meanwhile, I'm standing there contemplating the sheer magnitude of my folly thinking, "Now that was really, really stupid." Marielle showed up a bit later and confirmed my suspicions by telling me that it was, in fact, really, really stupid.

The pile never did ignite, so I had to get the rest of our community to help me with getting rid of it and keeping the dam busted down until we could get the hay off the fields.

Ron and the False Solomon Seal

    Ron and his girlfriend were going to have supper with us one spring night. Before coming over, they went for a hike in the woods to look for some false Solomon Seal shoots. It is what some call wild Asparagus. In the spring, False Solomon Seal shoots are very tasty. It was one of our favourite spring delights.

    When they arrived at our place, Marielle prepared to cook it. She noticed that it was not like she remembered but didn't say anything. At supper, I took one bite of it and spit it out. It was extremely bitter. Ron did the same. The girls didn't even try after seeing us spit it out. We threw it in the garbage and finished our meal.

    I forget why but Ron and his girlfriend had to leave early and we went about cleaning the dishes. I was cleaning up the table when I felt a sudden and excruciating pain in my stomach. I took another step and fell to my knees, screaming in pain. I then fell on the floor in a fetal position and thought I was going to die. It felt like someone had shoved a red-hot sword in my gut and was turning it around.

Needless to say, we decided we had to get to the hospital in Quesnel right away. How we got there, I have no idea. I just remember being there and so was Ron. We were both in ICU and trying to explain what had happened but neither of us could remember the name of the plant we had bitten into.

There is a plant that grows in the wild that looks almost identical to False Solomon Seal. It is one of the most deadly plants out there.

The hospital phoned the poison control unit at St Paul's hospital in Vancouver and eventually came up with the name of the plant and the antidote. The plant's name is False Hellebore and the antidote is Atropine. Atropine is derived from a poisonous mushroom called Amanita Muscaria. One poison is alkaline and the other is acidic. The result of combining them is a harmless salt.

They shot us up with the Atropine and we began to feel better. I was practicing Foot Reflexology at the time and started massaging Ron's feet. Suddenly my thumbs lost control. They bent back almost to my wrist. Then my legs got wobbly and then my arms. It was like all my tendons became like soft rubber. I couldn't even stand up. A nurse had to help me onto the bed. It was the strangest sensation. It eventually went away and Ron and I were released to our respective mates and went home.

So be careful folks, when foraging for wild foods. Know your plants: edible and poisonous. You never know when it will come in handy.

The Power of Water

    Our cabin was beside the Cottonwood River. There was a settling pond next to it with a berm separating the pond from the river. Just upstream was a narrow cut in the rocks that ice would jam up in, in the spring. Sometimes that dam would back up a lot of water. A short ways past the cabin, the river made a sharp angle bend to the right and that was where I would go to watch the show.

    Just about every year I would awake around 5 a.m. to the sound of massive flows of ice and rocks rumbling down the river, shaking the cabin. I would run down to the river and watch the water and ice rush by. Huge trees, 100+ feet long, with massive root balls would float on by at great speed and chunks of ice 30 feet around, 3 or 4 feet thick, would tumble end over end. It was a spectacular sight.

    One year the water came up so fast that I had to run as fast as my feet would carry me, back to the cabin, with the water lapping at my heels. The water stopped rising just a few feet short of the cabin. That could have been a disaster.

Goat Tails

BJ's Goat Horn

I was visiting BJ's trap line one day and he had a problem to solve that he needed my help with. It seems that whoever budded the goat's horns, usually done when they first start to appear, botched the job. This thick horn had grown up and turned down and was now pressing on the goat's skull causing it some aggravation. BJ wanted to remove the horn before it pierced her skull but needed someone to hold her still while he sawed it off.

Most people don't know this but a horn cut close to the skull leaves a really big hole in their skull that pumps out gallons of blood in a very short time unless the bleeding is stopped immediately. The other thing most people don't know is that spider webs will stop the bleeding immediately. BJ just happened to have a jar full of spider webs handy for just such an occasion. He had been collecting it for some time because there was a lot of it in the quart canning jar.

    I had never witnessed this operation before, although I had lived on a farm during my teen years, so I was not prepared for the amount of blood that came gushing out of her skull. With the deftness of a surgeon, BJ grabbed a handful of spider web from the jar and slapped it on the wound. The bleeding stopped immediately, much to my surprise and relief. She did not bleed for more than a few seconds.

    Good thing to know if you ever cut yourself real bad and need to stop yourself from bleeding to death. A jar of spider web should be in everyone's medicine cabinet.

My Goat's Horns

I was living in the bush when I got my goats as very young kids. I decided that they needed their horns to defend themselves against predators. It was a reasonable assumption at the time. And they grew up to need them on several occasions. But one was the alpha female and she was bossy, to say the least. She would attack any female, of any species, that entered her territory.

One day I looked out the window just in time to see a two and a half year old girl walk into our yard. I instinctively bolted out the door and stopped the goat just in time. Before I could act, I saw the girl squat down and pick up something and put it in her mouth. She screwed up her face and looked at me and said, "is no raisin". Some life lessons are harder than others.

That winter we had some visitors, one of whom was an eight month pregnant young lady. I don't remember why but we were trudging along a very narrow path in the snow going towards the river. The alpha female was in front of her and I was behind her. Suddenly the goat swung her head around and tried to spike the woman in the stomach.

    I reached around her, grabbed the goat's horn half an inch from her stomach. I flipped the goat up and over the woman and dropped her down on the trail upside down, jamming her horn into the compact snow. Don't ask me how I did it. I really didn't think it was possible but I guess I had such an adrenaline rush that I momentarily had super human strength.

    I decided that her horns, that were long and pointy, need a trimming; aka: cut the tips off. I had built a goat stanchion to hold them in while milking, so I wrestled her in there and went in search of my hacksaw. Marielle's brother was staying with us at the time, so I commissioned him into holding on to her horns while I did the cutting. He was a big city boy with no experience with animals and was very reluctant to get involved but I reassured him that it would be fine.

    I thought that all I needed was to take an inch or so off the tip to dull the horn, so I reckoned at which point the blood would reach so as to cause as little trauma to the goat as possible. I started to hack away and as the piece I cut fell away, a tiny little jet stream of blood shot up and landed right in my assistant's face. He started screeching like a banshee and let go of her horns. That screeching scared the crap out of the goat and made me laugh like an idiot.

    It took a while to convince him that we needed to cut the next horn and to get him to grab hold again. The goat was a little harder to convince but we eventually continued with the task at hand. I chose a spot just short of where I had cut the first one and was successful at avoiding spraying the brother this time.

I did have some spider web stashed in a jar for just such an occasion and was able to stop the flow on the first horn and didn't need any for the second one. But I don't think the brother ever forgave me. The goat didn't seem to mind much and we went about our co-existence quite fine after the ordeal.

Recently I saw that someone had stuck tennis balls on their goat horns. Looked pretty cool too. If I ever have to deal with goat horns again, I will use tennis balls.

Big John's Billy Goat

Big John was living on a hippie commune high up on the side of a mountain, east of Quesnel on the Quesnel

River. He had a billy goat that had a huge rack about six feet wide. It was a tough old goat and stank almost as bad as a skunk. But John loved that goat and used to take him everywhere he went, including in the passenger seat of his pickup truck.

I would occasionally go visit the commune, The Hill, and John. I was very good at trimming goat hooves and everywhere I went I would look at the goats' hooves and if they needed trimming, I would whip out my trusty Swiss Army Knife and start trimming. The first time I visited John and his goats, I went into the barn because it was kidding season and I wanted to see the kids.

I had heard that John's billy goat was an ornery old cuss, so when I was in playing with the kids, I saw the Billy approaching the door from the outside. I was like, "Oh Shit!" and took a flying run at the door. The goat's horns were too wide for him to just walk right in. He had to turn his head to do that. As I got to the door, I reached up my arms, grabbed the door jam, lifted my feet and smashed him in the head as hard as I could with my heavy work boots.

He took a step back, turned his head and got up on his hind legs and looked at me as if to say, "So, you want to play do you?" Don't ask me how I avoided being gored by that monster but somehow I did manage to get the hell out of there alive. Again, I think adrenaline was a major factor.

Anyway, a few years later, John had to go back to the states to get married and asked a neighbour to look after his goats. The guy soon realized that the Billy wanted to take him out. He somehow managed to get a chain around Billy's neck that was tied to a log. It took about a day before the Billy was dragging it around as if it wasn't there, so he added another log. This went on for a few weeks and he kept adding logs but it only slowed old Billy for a short time and it was back to normal.

Then he got the call that John was on his way home, so the goat sitter decided he needed to take the logs and chain off the goat because he knew that John would not be happy. I have no idea how he did it and lived but he did. John came home and everything looked Honky Dory and thought nothing of it.

John used to grab the billy by the horns whenever it got uppity, twist his head and flip him on his back, to establish that he was the alpha male.

So, the next morning, John goes out to the barn to check on the herd when in comes Billy and pins John into a corner. John wrapped his arms around Billy's horns and attempted to flip him over. Billy didn't budge. John realized that something was seriously wrong. I forget how he managed to get out of there but he was running for his house as fast as he could with Billy right on his ass.

He went up the front stairs and opened the front door. Just inside was a loaded 303 and he grabbed it, chambered a round, spun around and dropped Billy coming halfway through the door. He had shot his best friend and he was choked.

When he found out why Billy had been impossible to budge, it was all he could do to restrain himself from shooting the goat sitter. I visited him a few days later and heard the story. Shortly after that, Big John and his wife moved back to the States.

Stoned Goats

I was working on my truck one day when a friend came by to visit. I was up to my elbows in grease and crap from the 1948 Mercury pickup. My friend decided that I needed some relaxation and pulled out a glass vialof hash oil and placed it on the fender of the truck. He then reached into his pocket to bring out some rolling papers. As he did so, one of my goats jumped up on the fender and grabbed his vial.

She started chewing on the vial, crunching up with her teeth and swallowing it. My friend's eyes bugged out of his head. He said, "There was enough oil in there to get a couple of dozen people wasted. What do you think that will do to her?"

"Nothing." I said. "Goats are naturally stoned. It won't affect her at all."

"Well I don't see how that is possible. I'm gonna stick around and see how she reacts."

"Suit yourself but you will be wasting your time."

Nothing happened. He went away disappointed with one vial less in his stash.

Dog Bites Off Goat's Tail

I had my goats tethered in a field while I went to town one day. When I returned, I went to check on them and found that one was missing her tail. Well, at least the meat and fur were gone but the tailbone was still there. I found out it was the neighbour's dog that had attacked her.

I couldn't afford a vet, so I asked the local pharmacist what I should do. He said I had to cut off the bone as close as possible to her spine and to rough up the meat to make it bleed in order to sew up the wound. Not something I really wanted to do but it had to be done. The wound was pretty dry by the time I got all the stuff together: needles, thread, canning jar lid with a few dozen holes punched in it with a nail to scrape the wound raw, a block of wood as a chopping block and a sharp hatchet.

She was one strong and wild goat so I commandeered a few friends to lend me a hand. Three burly boys had to hold her down and still while I cut the bone off and scraped the wound raw. It took all they had to keep her down, especially when I cut the bone off. She almost threw them off. Once I had the wound raw, I had to sew her up. Not easy to do with all that fresh blood and raw meat. I did manage though, eventually. She spent that rest of her life as a Manx goat. Not too many of those around but she failed to see the humour in it.

Salmon Tails

My First Salmon

Living by the Cottonwood River was a godsend. Every mid-July, Spring Salmon would enter the river and congregate in the deeper pools, where they would stay until about mid September when they would leave the pools to spawn. One day, my friend was wandering around the bush and came across a pool with about 200 salmon swimming around the bottom. He rushed home and told us that it was going to be a full moon that night and that we were going to return to the pool to snag us some of them monsters.

Spring salmon can be between 35 and 65 pounds each. One salmon could be enough to get a body through the winter. Every fall, my wife and I would can up a few dozen half pint jars to get us through the winter. But this was my first winter and I did not have a wife, so I canned the salmon by myself.

That night we made our way out to the pool in the bright moonlight. We could see the dark shadows of the salmon as they meandered around the bottom of the pool. We put large lead weights on the ends of our lines and three treble hooks spaced about a foot apart. The idea was to have enough weight to cast to the far side of the pool and then drag it slowly until we felt it snag onto a fish, and then snap the rod up to set the hook.

The pool was too small to have more than two lines in the water at one time but there were four of us, so two had to wait on the sidelines for a turn. If one of us snagged one, the other had to reel in as fast as possible, so the lines didn't get tangled.

In short order, I snagged one. What a fight! I had never caught a fish this big in my life. It was all I could do to hang onto it. Every once in a while it would leap up out of the water and dance on its tail. It took me three quarters of an hour to land that monster.

I no sooner got it on shore than Jim cast his line out. Just as he did, a small cloud covered the moon and it got a little dark out. We couldn't see into the water. Suddenly his line started to race back and forth across the pool with amazing speed. A few minutes later, we could see a dark shadow surface and then there was a snort. We looked at each other; "Fish don't snort!" we chimed in unison.

Apparently there was a river beaver down there swimming among the 200 or so salmon. The moon came out from behind the cloud and we could see its shape. River beaver are quite a bit larger than pond beaver, like about twice the size. This one looked to be about 80 pounds. We knew there was no way this monster was ever going to let us land it and if we did it would never let us unhook it without it taking a few pounds of our flesh at the same time.

The beaver decided it didn't want anything to do with us and made a lunge for the outlet of the pool. It hit the fast water and ran out the line until it snapped off the end of the spool. There was nothing we could do. We felt bad that the beaver took all that line with a hook stuck in his hide. Chances are that it could die all tangled up in it. We packed up my fish and made our way back home.

Nonetheless, every September, I managed to score another salmon to get us through the winter. The next year I shot one with a 303 carbine, sitting on top of a small rise, overlooking the river. A friend was waiting down near the water and ran out and grabbed it as it floated by. The next year I got one with a bow and arrow. Both are very good stories.

My Second Salmon

My friend Pat (the ex-junky) and I set a date to go get our salmon for the year. The day before, Pat was driving his old Chevy pickup south toward Williams Lake from Quesnel, when he came to a long, fast curve in the road. Barreling toward him was a transport truck pulling a long mobile home. Somehow the back end of the trailer broke loose and swung out in front of Pat's truck. There was no way to avoid a collision. If he stayed in the truck, there was a 100% chance that he would be decapitated, so he bailed out.

    He jumped out of his truck at 60 miles an hour. His truck cut that trailer almost in half. Pat walked away with some pretty severe road rash but neither the truck nor the trailer survived. So I was stunned the next morning when Pat showed up at my door ready to go get some salmon.

    We went to a spot down river where it was shallow and fast. The salmon had already left the pools and were in the process of spawning. We chose a spot where a Cat pushed a cut on the bank where a small island of land stood beside the river. On top of this island was a small coniferous tree. The top of the island was barely big enough for the three of us (Pat, me and the tree).

    We watched as the fish spawned and when one had finished, she would rise up to the surface and struggle over to some small pool to await death. I shot her in the head. Pat was so excited; he leaped back and fell eight feet onto his back. I saw the pain in his eyes. Not only did he hurt his back in the fall but he fell on his road rash. Again I was surprised when he jumped up and ran down the river a few hundred yards and was able to catch the salmon before it was swept away by the current.

Another Salmon

The following year I decided to use my long bow. I taped a fishing reel to the bow, fastened an eye hook on the end of an arrow and set off to try this new method of fishing. Unfortunately, I did not do sufficient research on the subject and I did not adequately fasten the line to the arrow.

There was a gravel island in the middle of the river and my friend Johnny set up watch there with his big fish net. I was upstream a little and saw some salmon spawning in a shallow pool. I watched as she laid her eggs and the male fertilized them. When she was done, she moved away from the spot and I was able to get a shot in.

Never having done this before, I missed because of the diffraction of the water. It took me about ten shots before I got it right and I nailed her. She took off like a bat out of hell upstream. The arrow snapped and came floating back to me without the head. I trudged through the river, back to where Johnny was waiting. I was about to tell him to look out for her when he pointed upstream and shouted, "Would you look at that!"

    I turned and saw this salmon racing down stream at full tilt boogie, straight at us. She ran right up onto the end of the island and fell over on her side, dead. We stood there for a few moments staring at her in disbelief. Finally, I came to my senses and took out my knife to gut her. What I found was, there was no arrowhead in her but her heart was cut in four equal pieces. My arrow hit a perfect bulls eye but it had somehow worked its way out of her body while she was racing up and down the river. And she was gone for a good five to ten minutes.

    I knew the bullseye had nothing to do with skill. So I have to assume that the gods/goddesses wanted me to have that salmon and assisted in my aim.

Gnome Hunting

In 1975 I found a hard cover copy of The Gnome Book. It is an amazing piece of history and culture of Gnomes with wonderful water colour paintings by a Dutch master. At the beginning of the book is a series of maps showing the locations of where they live in the world. Just so happened that it indicated that gnomes lived in the North Cariboo region where we were. The other region where they live is here in the Kootenays where I live now.

After reading the book, Marielle and I decided to go out into the forest to see if we could find some. We wandered about for a few hours but all we saw were the occasional flashes of movement out of the corners of our eyes. When we turned to look, they would disappear. We decided to return to our cabin, disappointed.

    When we left the cabin, nobody knew we were gone and we didn't know how long we would be hunting gnomes, so nobody knew when we would return, not even us. So imagine our surprise when we walked through the door to find fresh pot of steeping tea and the table set with cups and saucers, cream and honey and a clean tablecloth. I believe the gnomes were saying "Hi" in their own little way… OK, a big way. We were probably not ready to see them or they were not ready to expose themselves to us but they wanted us to know that they were there and watching over us.

Department of Lands and Forest Decide to Evict all the Squatters

Around 1978, the Ministry of Forests, or as I prefer to call them, The Ministry of Deforestation, put out a report called the Trespass Cabins of Cottonwood. In this report were listed around 40 cabins with the names of their inhabitants. My cabin location was listed but it said the occupier was unknown. I thought, "Wow, I'm free." Turns out, I was just never around when they came to my cabin, so they never got to talk to me about it.

About that time I started working for the department of Holidays (Highways). At coffee break one day, a guy from the Lands Department came in and walked right up to me. "I just realized that you are the one who lives in the cabin down by the river in Cottonwood. I am here to tell you, (at this point he pulled out a Bic lighter and flicked it to flame) I am going to burn your cabin down at the end of the month."

I looked at him incredulously and said, "Your lighter is no competition for my 303." He stepped back stunned. I added, "You cannot burn my stuff. It is illegal." He said that I had to remove my stuff so he could burn my cabin. I said, "No. You come near my cabin with that lighter and I will shoot you." He went away but came back a few days later.

"I have ordered a Cat to go down there and push your cabin down."

I said, "You better tell the operator to wear a bullet proof vest."

He said, "I am sending two RCMP officers to accompany him."

I said, "You had better tell them to wear bullet proof vests too." (This was before it was mandatory for them to wear them).

I then went to the Government Agent and asked how I could get rid of this weasel. He said, just get a copy of the British North American Act and wave it in his face. Squatters built this country and it is written right in the Act that it is perfectly legal. I never did get a copy but the next time the weasel came around to harass me, I told him what the Government Agent old me. His eyeballs nearly popped out of his head. "My boss told you that?"

I said,"Look, I am not squatting on Crown Land." HE said, "How do you figure that?"

"You guys never signed any treaties with the Indians, so you are squatting on their land."

He tried to say something else, so I interrupted him and said, "Look, I am on the board of directors of the Native Friendship Center and I have their permission to live here. If you really want to piss me off, keep this up. I will get the Council of BC Indian Chiefs on your case."

He looked stunned and said, "Don't do that."

"Yup, now piss off and leave me alone." He never did try to speak to me again.

They ended up burning down over 40 cabins in the area. All those cabins were on mining claims or trap lines and the occupants were living there with permission from the owners. But, when the government tells you you have to move out, you think automatically that they have the authority to do so. I was the only one who refused. And I was the only one who was actually squatting on "Crown Land". Being an anarchist has its rewards.

When we moved out to the farm, we made sure that the friends who moved into our cabin would keep up the fight. Eventually, the area was claimed by a fellow who wanted to placer gold mine the area, and my friends had bought into a piece of land down river from there. They had some other friends come and dismantle my cabin and use the wood in their own cabins, so who knows if parts of it still live on.

Tough Love

(Joe Bfstplk was a character from the old Li'l Abner comics)

     One year Marielle's brother came to live with us for a while. He was what I would call a Joe Bfstplk kind of guy. He always had a dark cloud hanging over his head. Everyday it was, "Woe is me. The Universe is crapping on my head and from a great height." And everyday I would give him a pep talk to try to get him to see the brighter side of things. He couldn't get a job if his life depended on it. I tried to show him that it was his attitude that was keeping a job out of reach.

One day I came home from work at the local Department of Holidays (highways) to find Marielle sitting at the table crying. I inquired as to the cause of her grief. She said that her brother was driving her crazy. I said it sounds like time for tough love.

As we sat down to supper, in walks Joe Bfstplk, dragging his feet with an utter dejected look on his face. "The Universe is crapping on my head. Nothing is working out…"

I got up from the table, reached up to my 303 hanging on the wall, went over to the cabinet where my bullet clip was, popped it in the rifle, and chambered a round. I handed him the gun and said, "Here, go blow your fucking brains out and do everybody a favour."

He looked at me stunned, refused to take it, stepped back and mumbled something about he couldn't do that. I said, "Good. Smarten up then."

He packed up his stuff and drove back to Montreal, found Jesus, got a job and married a wholesome born again French girl that his parents approved of. We were happy and he was happy and we all lived happily ever after… until we didn't.

Bear and Fish Tales

Bear Tails

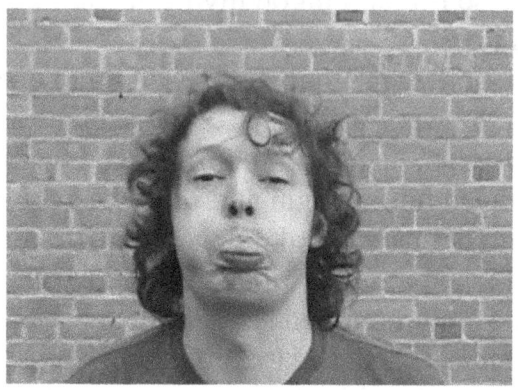

When we were living on our farm, I had an old Honda 350 enduro (dual sport) motorcycle. I was in town one day and I was riding home. The road was rough so I was standing on the foot pegs and letting my legs absorb the impacts of potholes and rocks. I came upon a truck with two guys, with their rifle dangling out the windows, creeping along at a slow pace, looking out for bear on the road. I slipped past them and picked up my pace.

I had in mind that, if I saw a bear, I would chase it off before these yahoos could get a shot off. I went about 7 or 8 miles on and, wouldn't you know it, there was a two year old black bear munching on the grass at the side of the road.

As I approached, I honked my horn and yelled at him/her. But it didn't even look up. I pulled over, stopped, put my feet down on the ground and started yelling at it to get off the road. It still didn't acknowledge my presence. So I put my kick stand down and stepped off my bike and said, "you had better get the hell out of here before those Yahoos get here and shoot you!" There was still no reaction.

At that point I could hear the truck approaching from around a bend in the road. So I stepped away from my bike and ran at the bear, which still had its head down munching on grass, and kicked it square in the butt. That got its attention and it ran off into the bushes. Before I could cross the road, the truck came into view and I stood there, put my thumb to my nose and waved my fingers at them while sticking out my tongue, "pllltttzzz!!!" as they drove by. They looked at me like, "what the hell is that crazy hippie doing that for?" Little did they know.

The Dead Bear

When we lived in the cabin down by the Cottonwood River, a friend, Don, decided to build a cabin off in the woods part way down to our cabin. One day, in spring, I was walking down our driveway and chanced to look over at his place. He wasn't home. He had an Akita dog and the doghouse was before his cabin. There was a bear with his head inside the doghouse eating the dog food. The Akita was on the end of a 10-foot chain, straining at the chain, freaked out of its mind.

I yelled at the bear but it paid me no attention. I ran down to my cabin to get my rifle. I ran back and ran at the bear but it took off into the woods. I ran after him. He only ran a hundred yards or so and stopped. He had run through a small indent on the ground and sat on a stump, looking back at me.

I looked at him for a few minutes and said, "You're not going to leave, are you?" He just sat there and made some noises as if talking to me. I said, "I need the meat. Are you here to sacrifice yourself so I can feed my family?" He mumbled something back then lowered his head. I said, "If I shoot you like that I will ruin a bunch of meat. Would you mind looking to the side?" He turned his head and I shot him through the eyeball.

    He was a 3 or 4 year old and weighed about three hundred pounds or more. I was thinking that I needed help getting him out of the woods. I started to walk back to my cabin when all of a sudden there was a van coming down the driveway with a friend at the wheel. I said, "What luck. I need a hand getting a bear I just shot out of the woods." He said fine and we set off back to where the bear was.

    When we got there he gasped. The bear had three claws missing on one hand. I said, "That's odd." He said, "Yes it is. Last fall I came home to my cabin (which was 30 miles away from ours) when I saw one of my windows was broken and there were three bear claws sitting on the window sill."

Bears and Fishing Tales

One of my passions was fishing. We practically live on fish. One of my favourite methods of fishing involved the use of a skidder tube. They are about 6 feet around and two people can straddle them like a horse, one on either side. We used to float down the Cottonwood River using canoe paddles to navigate. I had a telescoping rod and a backpack for my gear.

One day my brother and I were floating along to one of my favourite pools (the one where I caught my first salmon). The river went into a narrow spot with a high bank on the left and a gravel bar on the right, made a sharp right hand turn just before the pool. As we went into the narrow part, a young bear was walking along the ridge and as we went by it, it decided it wanted to be on the other side. It jumped right behind us onto the gravel bar.

My brother didn't want anything to do with it, so he insisted that we land on the far side of the pool. I wanted to fish off the gravel bar because the fish preferred that side of the pool. So I dropped him off on the far side and walked back up stream to a shallow spot to cross. I came to where I thought was the best place to cast my line from, and proceeded to assemble my gear to begin fishing. First cast I caught a nice rainbow trout. I unhooked it and placed it on the ground behind me and proceeded to make my next cast.

    I looked across the pool at my brother, who was jumping up and down, waving his arms frantically and pointing behind me. I couldn't hear him because of the roar of the river as it passed through the narrows but I could tell he was yelling. I looked behind me and saw the bear approaching my fish. I tried to shoo it away but it was not having any of that. It just kept coming at my fish. After a few attempts to get it to leave, I realized that it was not really afraid of me, probably because it had not encountered a human before.

    So I ran at it, yelling for it to go away but that failed too. Next, I ran at it and, as I closed the gap between us, it turned to walk away but I kept running at it and planted my boot squarely up its ass. That got its attention and it bolted out of there post haste. I calmly went back to fishing. My brother, on the other hand, was still jumping up and down, yelling at me. He seemed to be saying, "Are you crazy?" while pointing to his head and twirling his finger around the side of his head. I just smiled back at him.

Another time, Marielle and I were floating along, leaving a pool, and the river was wide, shallow and slow moving. On the left was a large raspberry patch and I could hear something shuffling about in the bushes. I knew it was a bear but its attention was on berries, so I knew it wasn't a problem… until, out of the forest on our right came running a tiny young bear cub bawling for its mommy.

I looked at the berry patch and back at the cub and knew that now we were in trouble. I said to Marielle, "Let's get the hell out of here. Paddle as fast as you can!" As we glided out of harm's way, I looked back and saw the Mamma Bear jump into the river and run across to her cub. We narrowly escaped a potentially dangerous situation because instinct took over: an instinct that did not exist in this big city boy a few years earlier.

The Alternative Intentional Community

In the Beginning

Around 1976, we decided that we needed to have some property to build more permanent stuff on, so we held some meetings in our tipi, with fellow bush hippies, with plans to form an alternative intentional community (a fancy name for a commune but seeing as most communes didn't last very long, we chose a more uppity name). Once we had a core group of eight, we set off to find the ideal piece of property.

My friend Dave and I worked at the Department of Holidays at the time, where they had a huge wall map of the surrounding area, with all the lot numbers. We found a lot out in the middle of nowhere that had three creeks running into it and one flowing out. The creeks formed four meadows. We found out that the piece was for sale and gathered up the crew on a Saturday and made the thirty miles trek up a logging road and three miles back in the bush.

We all fell madly in love with the place and the more we explored around, the more we loved it. We made plans, we dreamed, we discussed and we dreamed some more. When we saw it was getting late, we started to leave but as we crossed the last meadow, we saw several other people walking onto the land. We sauntered out to our vehicles and took off like bats out of hell, racing toward town. We got to the real estate office just as they were about to close at 5 pm. We slapped some cash on the guy's desk and we closed the deal in about half an hour.

It was 106 acres surrounded by "Crown Land" and with good water flow… and the price was right; $19,500. How could we go wrong? But we did…

Having been brought up in suburbia, most of us didn't have a clue what it meant to live communally; what was involved in living with eight emotionally challenged adolescent adults. It was like being married to seven other people. None of us was mature enough to weather that storm.

It didn't take long before the power struggles and infighting started. And we were too far out in the bush to get away from each other to get some perspective.

It took three years before most of us were living out there full time and by then, three of the original members had backed out, leaving only five adults. That winter was the ball breaker.

Dave was a major stoner and just wanted to bake bread and eat it. He would not participate with common chores, like bringing in the hay or gardening. He always had an excuse. Finally, his partner had had enough and walked across the meadow and moved in with BJ, whose partner had left him a year earlier, when they were still living out on the trap line.

The Pigs

One day BJ showed up with three pregnant sows and a scrawny boar. We had no fencing for them so he just turned them loose. Eventually we built a log pen for the boar in the middle of the first meadow but the sows just wandered off into the forest. We would put food out for them to keep them close to the farm. These sows must have weighed close to 600 pounds each, so we didn't worry about them much, even though we were way out in the bush.

We would go out every once in a while to check on them and they were doing fine, even though we saw bear tracks in the same mud puddles as there were pig tracks. Those sows could rip a bear apart with their powerful jaws. We had no problem with bears ever. Then the time came to drop their piglets.

We had to build farrowing pens for them. But first we had to build a large pen to keep them in. I went to the West Fraser sawmill and bought a sling of 2" X 10" reject lumber for $40. We bush Hippies used to buy many of those slings to build most everything we needed. A sling is 4' X 4' X whatever length you needed.

I do not recommend trying to herd three huge sows. It was quite the chore, almost as hard as herding cats. By now they were wild, feral beasts and did not want to come in. We had built a large pen with a wide gate to keep them in. Dave was holding the gate open when we tried to get the sows in but one of them decided to fight back.

As she was going through the gate, she charged Dave and ran toward his crotch. I never saw a human jump so high before. He went straight up in the air about eight feet. It was a good thing too, as she lifted her head as she went between his legs and tried to bite his balls off. It took him a few days to come down off the adrenaline rush. We eventually got them penned up and settled in.

The neighbours had borrowed BJ's billy goat to breed one of their does and I was visiting them one day. They asked me to return the goat to BJ because it was really sick, so I loaded it into my truck and drove up to our place. The goat looked like it was on its last legs. I suspect it had eaten too much grain and was bloating. BJ was at home across the meadow, so I looked and there were no pigs in sight, so I put that goat just inside the pen gate and ran across the meadow to get BJ.

When we got back to the pen, the pigs had already half eaten the goat from the ass end up. It was still alive but barely. We shot him in the head to put him out of his misery then left him there for the pigs to finish off.

The boar was in the pen in the middle of the first meadow all by himself. The log fence around him was about five feet tall. The previous owner had not removed his tusks when he was young and they were as sharp as razors. One day I was trying to pour his food over the fence, where the feed trough was, but he stood up on the fence with his front legs and blocked my way. I had on one of those mesh gloves that tree fallers wore that were supposed to stop an idling chain on a chainsaw. So I smacked him on the face to get him to move.

When I looked down, my hand was bleeding like a stuck pig. His tusk had cut the glove wide open and the palm of my hand with it. He didn't get fed right then as I had to beeline it back to the house to stop the bleeding. It was a few hundred yards back to the house. I had not collected any spider web. We had to bandage the wound as best we could and make the 35 mile journey to the Quesnel hospital to have it sewed up.

BJ drove me to the hospital. While he was waiting for me to get patched up, he went shopping and bought a six-pack of ice-cold beer. The doctor asked me if I was allergic to anything and I told him Zilocane. He sewed me up without anesthetic. When I got to BJ's truck I was in a lot of pain and he had a six-pack of anesthetic sitting right there. I chugged two or three beer before I was sufficiently anesthetized.

Shortly after that, I traded the boar for a Savinios Wind Spinner.

(https://www.motherearthnews.com/renewable-energy/savonius-super-rotor-zmaz74zhun).

(Copy and paste the URL into your browser window to see what it is.)

Just after we had the farrowing pens built, the sows decided to drop their loads. BJ had rigged up a propane heater to keep the piglets warm as it was late fall. One morning, about three weeks later, I heard a loud bang and a hissing sound, like a jet taking off. I ran down to the pen to see the sow had knocked the heater over; the hose was burned in half and flames were shooting out of the hose. The piglets were being fried. I tried to turn off the propane, but I burned my hand real bad, and had to use a rag to turn off the valve.

By this time, BJ had come up from his place but we only managed to save four or five of the piglets. Most of them were missing tails and ears and were suffering from severe burns. The rest were toast. We were able to treat the burns and a few of them survived long enough to make it to our stomachs. They were quite tasty: partially pre-cooked as they were.

What? I warned you at the beginning of this book.

BJ's Jersey Cow

On another day, BJ showed up at the community with a Jersey cow. He didn't tell us that he was going to get it, but nobody objected as she was in full milk production. I would say that her milk was about 30% cream. I would make butter from it and we had all the milk and cream three families could handle and then some. We would feed the excess milk to the pigs.

A few months later I saw BJ walking the cow down the driveway at dusk. Our driveway was 3 miles long and our nearest neighbour was another mile farther up the Garner Road. I was curious why he was walking with the cow in tow. When I inquired, he said, "She's in heat. I'm taking her down to the neighbour's bull."

Our neighbour had a prize wining Angus bull that was worth a hell of a lot of money and he charged an arm and a leg for his services. I'm like, "How can you afford that?" He said he couldn't and that is why he was going down there at night. He also said the neighbour was not at home and what he didn't know, wouldn't hurt him. I should have known right then and there that BJ and I would clash on a lot of issues.

Anyway, I was busy with other problems and let it slide. In the morning, the cow was happily grazing in our meadow and I didn't give it another thought. She eventually produced a pure Angus bull calf. At about a year old, that bull must have weighed in at 5 or 6 hundred pounds. I had left the farm for a year after my run in with the logging truck but found out later, that Dave had trained the bull to pull logs out of the bush. He called him Bob. Everybody who visited the farm loved Bob.

Every year around Thanksgiving we would hold a badminton tournament and a feast. In 1981, Dave had spit roasted two lambs. Everybody got so drunk and stoned that nobody bothered with protocols and just ripped off chunks of meat and ate like cave men. Tin 1982, Dave barbequed beef. Everybody was enjoying the meal when someone asked where Bob was. "You're eating him" came Dave's dry retort. Some people took offence, some gagged, one person threw up but most said, "Bob tastes great." Such was life on the farm.

The Logging Truck Incident

I was flat broke, it was the middle of February, and my wife was getting upset because we had a seven-month-old son, 30 miles out in the bush with no income at all. Not too well planned! Then each of the other three land partners came to me with their tales of woe to cry on my shoulder and make excuses for their behaviour. I was overwhelmed with the responsibility that everyone was dumping on my shoulders. I remember standing out in the snow all alone and screaming at the sky, "Get me out of here. I can't take this any more."

The next morning, I set out on my antique snowmobile to go down to our nearest neighbour's house to see if I could get a ride to town. I was planning to go to welfare to see if I could get some assistance. Turned out, they were planning to go the following day, so I set off for home after a short visit.

It had not snowed for quite a while and the road and their driveway were solid compact snow and ice. The end of their driveway came out onto the road in the middle of a hairpin turn. When I got to the end of the driveway, I planned to swing up onto the snow bank to go the mile to our driveway.

When I tried to stop the snowmobile, it just kept sliding on the ice and I ended out on the road just as a logging truck was going by. The muffler on my machine was shot and so noisy that I didn't hear the logging truck coming.

All I remember seeing was this great big chrome bumper and the lights went out. I felt like I had exited my body on impact. I remember looking down on my body from above and the people that suddenly appeared out of nowhere. I saw the neighbour's wife shaking me and asking if I was OK. Her shaking was causing me a lot of pain so I re-entered my body and said, in a very strained voice, to please stop shaking me and then exited my body again.

I lay on the ice for over an hour waiting for an ambulance. Nobody would move me until the ambulance arrived. The ambulance took off toward town but the road was so bumpy from being pounded by logging trucks that they stopped about a mile down the road and called in a helicopter. I was weaving in and out of consciousness. When I was loaded on the helicopter, I realized that this was the first copter ride of my life, so I tried to look out the window but I kept slipping back into unconsciousness.

I was unconscious when we landed at the Quesnel airport where they transferred me to another ambulance for the few miles to the hospital. Somehow Marielle and my son got there before me. When they were transferring me from the ambulance gurney to the hospital gurney, the two slipped apart and they dropped me on the hospital floor. Marielle was there to witness this debacle and went ballistic on them. She told me about it later.

It seemed that the father of the truck driver somehow made it out to our farm and rescued her and my son while I was being transferred from one vehicle to another, to another.

Anyway, I ended up in the emergency ward. That night I was in a room that was constantly monitored, with all the lights on. It was very weird. Every hour on the hour I would descend into the light. There were all these faces of people wearing white so all I really saw were faces in the light. I would pop open my eyes and look at the clock; 1 am, 2 am, 3 am, 4 am… etc. When I awoke in the morning, I saw a nurse filling up a needle and I asked, "Is that morphine?" She said yes. I said, "I don't want any more of that shit." That was just too weird a trip.

For three days they didn't give me any painkillers. Finally, Marielle asked a nurse if they could give me something to help with the pain I was experiencing. They said, "but he refused morphine." She said, "Surely you have other forms of painkillers." It so happened that they did. Why they hadn't given them to me is still a mystery.

Eleven days later I said to Marielle, would you please bring three or four big guys with you tomorrow and get me the hell out of here. They are killing me with their drugs and bad food. Next day 3 big guys I know came and pretty much carried me out of the hospital.

They told me that I had to come in to the hospital for physio therapy. The first two visits were OK, as the therapist was gentle. My right arm was locked in an upright position with my hand up by the shoulder. I could not straighten it out.

It seems that while I was lying in the hospital those first twelve days, my tendons shrank. The therapist was gently trying to stretch the tendons so I could use my right arm again.

On my third visit, there was a different therapist. She took one look at my arm and said, "We have to get that straightened out right away." She told me to sit in a chair and put my arm up on the gurney that was beside the chair. She then grabbed my wrist and elbow and tried to wrench it straight.

Holy Hell! That friggin' hurt. After I peeled myself off the ceiling, I started screaming expletives at her, calling her every derogatory name I could think of. She could have torn all the ligaments and tendons in my arm. It felt like she had.

By this time, we had moved back out to the farm. I rigged a pulley up to one of the main beams in our ceiling, some rope with wooden handles and started pulling on my arm. It took me two months to straighten my arm out again. I never returned to physio.

I also built a sweat lodge down by the creek, where there was a pool. I would sweat every day for the next two months and soak in the ice cold water of the pool. The creek never saw sun light until it was well past the pool, so it was just above freezing until late summer.

The Teachings of Don Juan

Back in the 70s, I read just about every one of Carlos Castaneda's books about Don Juan and the art of living in a sorcerer's world. I loved to experiment with those teachings. I was out in the forest with Marielle and a friend one day when the opportunity presented itself to try one such experiment.

We came upon a rather large tree that had fallen over. It had been uprooted and the roots were still intact. It had fallen uphill, so the ground fell away from the roots. I ran up the trunk of the tree and up onto the roots. Up there, it looked like the ground was about 15 – 20 feet down, slanting down hill. I thought about how Don Juan had said that you can do super human stuff with the right attitude.

So I squatted down, took several deep breaths and jumped. I landed really hard. But I didn't wrench any joints or pull any tendons.

I was sore, and a little stunned, but still functioning. I remember that he also said to use sound to add power to any such activity, so I went back up onto the root ball, and decided to try adding sound to my jump. I squatted down, took several deep breaths, let out a mighty scream and jumped. I literally floated down to the ground and landed as light as a falling leaf. It was incredible. I was elated. My companions were amazed.

A little while later, that same afternoon, we came upon another fallen tree, only this one had fallen downhill over an old logging road. I could walk under the trunk without having to duck at all. I looked up at the trunk. It seemed to be close to 20 to 24 inch in diameter. I squatted down again, took several deep breaths and let out a blood-curdling scream, and jumped up as hard as I could. Damned if I didn't land on the trunk with both feet. Again my friends were amazed. I was amazed.

Don Juan also talked about the gate of power. It consisted of running in the forest, in the dark raising your knees to your chest. He also said that you would not collide with any object while running in such a manor. So, of course, I had to try it.

It is not as easy as it sounds, though. It takes a lot of practice to accomplish running while bringing your knees up to your chest. The first few time I ran into trees and received a goose egg on my forehead for my efforts. I never did master the gate of power but it was worth the try.

Drafting for the Department of Holidays

In 1976, I needed some cash flow, so I got a job at the Department of Holidays in Quesnel. My job was to draw the roads that the surveyors plotted out in the field. After living in the bush for four years, I was feeling rather claustrophobic sitting in an office everyday. I was there for about three months when I asked my stuporviser if he would please send me out with the survey crew so I could get some fresh air.

He reluctantly acquiesced and out I went. We were sent to a road near Dragon Lake just southeast of town. The road was straight except for a slight jog around a dip in the topography. We were to plot a line straight through the dip, which was about 6 meters deep and a hundred meters wide. I was sent down into the dip to make sure nothing obscured the line of sight. The head surveyor set up his transit at the edge of the dip.

As I walked down, I saw a sizable poplar tree that looked like it was in the way, so I sighted up at the transit and ascertained that it was, indeed, in the way. All they gave me to do this job was a very dull axe. So I started to chop away at the side toward which I wanted the tree to fall. When I thought that my cut was sufficient, I went to the opposite side to make my back cut.

The surveyor yelled down to me, "which way is that tree going to fall?" To me it was a stupid question because, if he knew anything at all about falling trees, he would see which way it was going to fall. So I, being the crazy that I was, told him it was going to fall in the opposite direction, which seemed to please him. I finished cutting the tree and it began to fall exactly where I wanted it.

I looked up as it went and noticed, for the first time, that it was going to fall across a power line. Ooops! So that is why he asked me which direction it was going to fall. Hindsight is 2020. Luckily I was standing on the only dry hump of land down there because the rest of the place was a swamp.

The power line broke and fell into the water and started flipping around, shooting sparks all over the place. It was better than fireworks. I was standing there, completely surrounded by water that was charged with enough electricity to fry my ass, but I was so in awe of the light show, that I didn't even think of the danger I was in.

The next thing I hear is the surveyor spinning his tires on the gravel road, spraying gravel all over the place, as he bee lined it out of there at mach speed. When the fireworks ended, I crawled up out of the hole I was in and sat on the edge to wait for the axe to fall. My friend Dave, who was also on this survey crew, came over and sat beside me and lit up a joint.

After a while, all the bigwigs showed up to survey the damage. I found out later that a couple of hundred houses were without power because of my little oops. I fully expected that I would be grounded and be stuck in the office for the rest of my tenure. But, low and behold, they let me back out with the survey crew the next day. I guess they found my little oops entertaining or something. I wasn't going to complain.

The next job I was on was a high-speed curve on the West Fraser Road. It was about a kilometer long. We were told to survey the centerline of the road. So we did and I drew up the plans back at the orifice. A few weeks later we were called back out to the road because something went terribly wrong.

It seemed that the road building contractor had started building the road from both ends of the curve at once but used the center line we surveyed as the outside of the road and they didn't meet at the center. The inside of one end of one was the outside of the other end. They tried to blame it on us but it didn't stick, of course. That was a level of oops that made mine look like a kindergarten oops. I believe it cost them a few million to fix.

Part 3

The Magic of Morley

Every end of July, the Stony Indian band, at Morley Alberta, would hold a ten day gathering called an ecumenical conference. It would seem that, at some point in the 1960s, the council of Canadian Christian Churches realized how badly they messed up the indigenous people, that they decided to try to rectumfy the situation.

They went in search of any native persons who still knew the traditional teachings. They only found nine people who were brave enough to admit they did, the first year. That gathering kickstarted the resurgence of the Native spiritual revival in North America.

In 1978 I was working at the Department of Holidays and was feeling rather discombobulated after six years in the bush. I was feeling disassociated from myself. I knew a Cree woman who lived in Quesnel, so I went to see her one day to ask if she knew of any medicine people in the area. She said there were none that she knew of but that she was going to Morley in a month or so and I was welcome to go too. So that is how I got to go to my first Native gathering.

My friend Debbie wanted to come along too, so I asked the Cree woman if that was OK. She said sure. While driving up the highway to Banff, we saw a bunch of cars parked on the side of the road up ahead where the Bow River runs beside the highway. I knew some animal was there and that the tourists had stopped to take pictures. When we arrived at the scene there was a long line of cars parked on the riverside and a high rock bluff on the other. Two Big Horn Sheep were descending onto the highway. I drove past all the cars and pulled over to take a better look.

As I turned to look back, the sheep had come up out of the ditch and stepped out onto the pavement. All the tourists ran and jumped into their cars. I stuck my head out of my window and called back to the sheep to please come up to my car so I could pay my resects. They did just that. One came right up to my window and stuck his head inside the car. I really had never seen one up close and was kind of surprised just how massive the head and horns are.

I stroked his head, spoke gently to him and told him how much I admired and appreciated his coming to visit me. Debbie was sitting there mumbling under her breath, "Holy Shit, Holy Shit!" It seemed like time stood still. The ram took his sweet time before leaving to continue on his mission. I don't know how long I sat there basking in such an amazing blessing. What a way to start a 10-day journey with indigenous peoples.

The man the Cree woman wanted me to meet was three days late arriving. Many of the spiritual elders did not want to share their pipes and ceremonies with the "white" people who were attending. (There were about 50 Caucasians present among four thousand indigenous peoples). When Albert Lightning arrived, a man told him what was going on and he called a special meeting of all elders in his tipi.

He told them that it doesn't matter what colour of skin, religious affiliations or economic status people have; if they come seeking knowledge, it is their duty to teach them. The world was in dire need of those teachings, especially the Caucasians. I watched as the elders came out of the tipi with their heads hanging low. This man was to become one of my teachers.

For the next seven days, I was immersed in the world of the indigenous people and their ceremonies. With each new experience, the intensity grew. I witnessed so much magic, so many new layers of reality, it was a life changing event. When I returned to my community, I told the stories of my experiences and everybody wanted to attend the following year. That was another adventure too.

Albert Lightning's medicine name was Buffalo Child. On the last day of the gathering I was so burned out that I couldn't pack my camping gear. I just wanted to sleep for days. It was so sunny and hot that I lay down beside my car to get some shade. As I looked up at the sky I saw a cloud form in the shape of a man dressed in a buffalo robe riding on the back of a buffalo. I got a sudden rush of energy and got up, packed my gear, and was off toward home, lickity split.

I knew that he was going to play a major role in my life. I would attend his ceremonies every chance I could.

A Magical Morley Experience

On the fourth night of the gathering of over four thousand participants, traditional drumming and dancing was scheduled. I was excited by the prospect of attending. I had never been to a Pow Wow before. Shortly after dark, I heard the singing and drumming start some distance from my camp. As I set out in the direction of the music, I looked up at the sky. It was very clear and the stars were many and bright. However, when I was halfway to the location of the Pow Wow, I noticed the air was beginning to vibrate, causing the stars to blur. Soon I saw the stars were obliterated altogether. This development only fueled my curiosity.

About three-quarters of the way to my destination and about a hundred yards to my left, up a small rise, was the site of the sacred fire. When I reached this point I stopped in my tracks. I was overwhelmed by a strong urge to go to the fire. I tried to ignore my inner voice. I remembered being told earlier that day, by one of the elders, to always heed this voice. Eventually I gave in, aborting my original mission, and went to the fire.

Upon arrival I saw an old Navaho Medicine man, his wife, and a young couple, each holding a child on their laps, sitting opposite each other around the fire. The old man was laying out his ceremonial paraphernalia in obvious preparation to perform traditional healing. I sat on the ground a short distance from them wondering why I had been summoned. The old man obviously knew what he was doing, but I had no experience in such matters. I was determined to find out, though.

Soon the preparations were complete. The old man turned to me and said that if I did not intend to stay until the end of his ceremony he would request I leave before he began. Leaving during the proceedings would disturb what he was trying to accomplish. I answered that I understood and would like to remain, if it was all right with him. He thanked me for staying, which puzzled me.

I also had no idea why or of what use I could possibly be. I was soon to find out.

Before he began, the voice in my head said I was not to watch because this was his Medicine and not for my eyes to see. I was sitting on the ground with my legs folded in front of me, so I closed my eyes and let my head drop forward. Almost immediately I heard a thunderous roar in my ears, like a rocket taking off, and a warm pressure at the centre of the top of my head. The pressure and noise increased until my head seemed to open up and a beam of light poured out. As the light grew brighter I 'saw' the beam go out across the fire and split in two. Each part of the beam then entered the foreheads of the two children. None of this did I will to happen, nor did I understand what was happening. The experience was so intense that I was unable to think at all.

This light was issuing forth from my head with such force that it was difficult to prevent myself from being pushed over backwards. It took considerable physical effort to hold myself steady so as not to deflect the beams away from their targets. I began to shake and sweat from the strain.

After what seemed like a very long time, the intensity of the light and noise began to fade, then stopped. I could no longer 'see' the children. Slowly I raised my head and opened my eyes but they fell shut instantly. I had only a brief glimpse of the scene before a new beam of light burst from my forehead accompanied by the roar of rocket engines, and went out across the fire as before. This time I found it more difficult to resist the backward push on my body. I was becoming exhausted and my clothes were damp with perspiration. I was beginning to get chilled in the cool mountain air. The pressure and intensity would not subside. All I could do was hold on.

After what seemed like an eternity, the light and noise stopped and I collapsed on my side, panting and sweating, too exhausted to open my eyes. I must have passed out or fallen asleep, for when I finally did open my eyes, I was alone. I had heard no one leave. I was too tired and cold to think or care about anything. I just wanted the warmth of my sleeping bag, which I had to crawl a quarter of a mile or so to get to.

The next day, I awoke with a clear understanding of the preceding evening's events. I had been used by the old shaman as a channel for the energy that had been concentrated in the area by the drummers and dancers. The energy had flowed through me in a focused form and passed on to the children. The ordeal was so hard on me because of the intensity of the energy harnessed and because I was not accustomed to being used as a channel.

Ed Loses His Way

The first time I went to the Morley gathering I spent the first three days wandering about aimlessly, not being able to make any connections or find any natives to talk to me, let alone teach me anything. I met several other 'white' people who were complaining about the same thing. One was a young man from northern Manitoba named Ed (not his real name). We would bump into each other occasionally and ask each other if we had found something - a teacher or an event to participate in. We agreed to let the other know if we did.

Then, early on the fourth afternoon, I spotted some native men working on something by the edge of a clearing at the far end of the camp. I walked over and inquired if they needed any assistance and they said they would welcome it. As it turned out, they were building a sweat lodge. This was a turning point - lesson number one. Now that I was not looking for what I could get out of it but offering to help, things started to come to me.

These men taught me how to build a sweat lodge and the fire to heat the rocks in their traditional way. When we were finished with the preparations for the ceremony, I was invited to return later to assist in it. I left feeling elated.

On my way back to camp I saw a group of people sitting in a circle at the edge of a ridge. They were listening to a woman talking. I sat down in the grass about fifty feet away, listening but pretending I wasn't. I was acting cool and disinterested but in fact I was feeling shy and unworthy of her knowledge.

What intrigued me was her ability to synthesize religious and spiritual knowledge from all over the world into one smooth flowing dialogue as if they all came from the same source - second insight! When she finished and everybody was leaving, she strolled right up to me, tapped me on the shoulder, looked me straight in the eye and said, "I think you are the person I was to contact today to give a message. I have no time right now but if you come to that tipi (pointing to it) at 7:30 tonight we will have more time to talk." Then she strolled away, leaving me sitting there, feeling like a complete dork.

Eventually, I bumped into Ed and told him what had happened, about being invited to a sweat lodge and the meeting with this woman afterwards. He had a completely uneventful day and was feeling quite depressed. When he heard my story he excitedly asked where the meeting was and if I minded if he tagged along. For some reason I was compelled to say that if he was meant to be there he would find a way to do so. I left him standing there looking very dejected.

    Later that night, sitting in the tipi, after finding out the Red Tailed Hawk was my spirit guide, I heard the door flap open. I turned to see Ed, with his eyes as big as saucers, with a smile from ear to ear. He was beaming like a halogen lamp saying, "I found it!" I smiled back and beckoned him to sit beside me. I asked how he found the place. He said he was wandering about in the dark, completely lost, when he tripped on a smoke flap pole from a tipi a little ways away. He lost his balance and lunged into some guy who was having a pee out back of the tipi.

    They both crashed to the ground in a heap. The other man yelled, "What the hell are you doing?" Dave replied, "I'm looking for knowledge." The man said "For crying out loud, it's the third tipi on the left."

    Life is kind of funny that way. Just when you figure you're lost in the dark some stranger tells you where to go.

The True Spirit of Christmas

In 1983, I was invited to a Winter Solstice ceremony on the Hobema Reserve south of Edmonton, Alberta. I was visiting my most revered teacher, Albert Lightning. At this event, attended by several hundred reserve residents, Albert conducted a traditional pipe ceremony. He blessed the huge piles of food, clothing, blankets, and other goods that had been assembled on the floor of the hall we were in.

Once blessed, all the goods were equally distributed to everyone in attendance. I was the only non-native there. I received one pile of goods and another of food. Then we had a great feast. Afterwards, a few dozen people stood in line to shake my hand and thank me for participating in their ceremony. To say that I was in shock and extremely blessed would be an understatement. Words just cannot express how honoured I felt.

This tradition dates back hundreds of years. When they would come together to make winter camp, they would put everything in the camp, except for the clothes on their backs, into piles at the center of the camp. To ensure that every member of the tribe had an equal opportunity to survive the winter, everything was equally distributed to all.

Does this sound like the actions of uncivilized savages? Look around at our "civilization" and ask yourself, Who really are the savages?

The Birth Of My Son

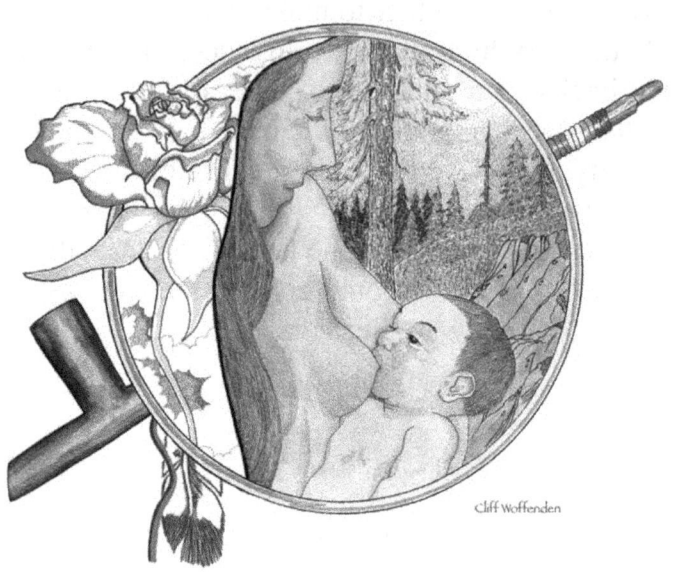

At one such ceremony, at the Fish Lake Cultural Center west of Williams Lake, Marielle and I sat in a sweat lodge with several other people. Marielle was about 4 months pregnant. During that sweat, Albert brought in the spirit of the Eagle. It passed from person to person, fanning them with its wings. The only things, besides hot rocks and bodies in there, were a small bucket of water and a birch switch to sprinkle water on the hot rocks.

When the Eagle came to Marielle, it brushed her belly with its wings. It circled the lodge 4 times and each time it brushed her belly.

On June 25th of that year, she gave birth to our son. I was standing beside her coaching her breathing when out popped his head. He turned his head, looked me straight in the eyes and said (telepathically) "Hi, I'm Eagle Child." I nearly fainted because I understood that a name with Child after it was a medicine name.

I did not want to give him a name. I wanted to ask Albert if he would give him a name when we attended the conference a month later. As it turned out Albert did not have permission to give a child a name. When we were at Morley, Marielle wanted to know how Eagle Child was pronounced in Cree. She went to Albert while he was setting up his tipi. He looked up at her (she was so white she could glow in the dark) a little angry. "Who gave him that name?" he demanded.

She told him the story of the birthing and he stood there for a minute contemplating what to do. Then he reached out his hand and placed it my son's forehead for a few minutes and nodded his head in the affirmative. He took out a small pad of paper and wrote his name in Cree and showed Marielle how to pronounce the name. She returned to our camp and told me what happened and how to pronounce his name.

I love the Cree language but I could not wrap my tongue around it. No matter how hard I tried, I just could not get it right. When Albert would pray or tell jokes in Cree, it was like singing. It has a lyrical quality to it. Marielle was from northern Quebec and she spoke a very old form of French and it had the same lyrical quality as Cree. I couldn't wrap my tongue around French either.

Postscript

Like I said, life in the bush is not for the faint of heart. There was much magic and spiritual enlightenment, good times, and not so good times, but it all was a learning curve for life. I set out to escape the madness of the big city and found that the madness was in me. Coming to terms with my own madness was, after all, the name of the game we all play.

I'm sure there are more stories hiding in the far reaches of my mind but I can't seem to reach them right now, so I will stop here.

I sincerely hope you enjoyed this romp through my past. It was fun digging through my memory banks to bring them out to you.

www.ingramcontent.com/pod-product-compliance
Lightning Source LLC
Chambersburg PA
CBHW061951070426
42450CB00007BA/1246